KU-606-398

# Generative
# Design

ASTERIOS AGKATHIDIS

LAURENCE KING PUBLISHING

# CONTENTS

## 1.0

INTRODUCTION TO
GENERATIVE DESIGN > 6

## 2.0

CONTINUOUS SURFACES > 22

## 3.0

MODULARITY AND
ACCUMULATION > 46

## 4.0

DEFORMATION AND
SUBTRACTION > 70

GENERATIVE DESIGN:
FORM-FINDING TECHNIQUES IN ARCHITECTURE

**LAURENCE KING**

Published in 2015 by
Laurence King Publishing Ltd
361–373 City Road
London EC1V 1LR
United Kingdom
enquiries@laurenceking.com
www.laurenceking.com

A catalogue record for this book is
available from the British Library

ISBN: 978 1 78067 691 3

Cover Design by Pentagram
Design by & SMITH

Printed in China

.

Asterios Agkathidis is Lecturer in
Digital Design at the Liverpool School
of Architecture. He is the author of
numerous publications, including
*Modular Structures* (2009) and
*Computational Architecture* (2012).

# 5.0

ALGORITHMIC PATTERNS > 90

# 6.0

TRIANGULATION > 116

# 7.0

CONCLUSION: THE DIGITAL
VS PHYSICAL DEBATE > 146

# INTRODUCTION TO
# GENERATIVE DESIGN

# 1.1 / DESIGN METHODS IN ARCHITECTURE: A BRIEF REVIEW

Generating form poses one of the fundamental questions in architectural education and practice. Architectural production is frequently accompanied by debates about the legitimacy of its design approach, questioning the relationship between function and form, aesthetics and construction systems, context and structure, user needs and construction costs, in all possible configurations.

In recent years, computational tools have introduced innovative form-finding techniques, revolutionizing architectural design and production. These techniques are often described by terms such as 'generative design', 'parametric design' or 'algorithmic design', to name but a few. These offer new design paths to architects by breaking with predictable relationships between form and representation in favour of computationally generated complexities, thus enabling the development of new topologies. They shift the emphasis from 'form making' to 'form finding' (Kolarevic 2003).

The critics of such design approaches claim that they disconnect architectural output from its context and its users, and lead to a decrease in spatial quality and a building's integration within the urban environment. Furthermore, some argue that a totally computerized approach leads to disconnection from physical modelling and drafting techniques – once essential foundations of architectural education – and so risks the loss of material qualities, effects and properties.

Yet various generative form-finding techniques existed in architecture long before the digital revolution. At the start of the twentieth century, many visionary architects, engineers and designers, such as Frederick Kiesler and Frei Otto, were applying design methods that were very similar to today's computational approach. It seems that today's new computational design techniques are not as new as they seem, nor impossible to practise without the use of computational tools. So is it the tools or the design method that should be targeted by critics of so-called digital architecture? The following will try to cast light on that perpetual conflict.

Why, though, should anyone follow a method for designing architecture in the first place? Can architects not simply rely on personal inspiration or their own sense of beauty? Throughout the evolution of architectural design there have certainly always been schools of thought that have encouraged a design process based on inspiration or an initial stimulus. However, others have promoted adherence to a specific design method, based on rules rather than intuition, and many now argue that design methods are necessary in order for architects to deal with today's hyper-complex design briefs, or to prevent self-indulgence and stylistically driven formal language. Others affirm that emerging computational design and fabrication tools are changing the architect's role, making design methods a necessity. In order to gain a better understanding of this debate it is worth briefly reviewing the various form-finding philosophies that have dominated architectural design over the past century and are still being widely used today.

## Design processes driven by nature

Looking back at pre-computational times, around the end of the nineteenth century, avant-garde architects and thinkers were starting to question the historicist architecture of their time, which they felt was immoral and anachronistic because it failed to reflect both technological evolution and social structure; it did not correspond to the zeitgeist. They started to urge for universal design principles that would replace individual taste and the mere reproduction of historical styles. In their attempt to do so, their attention turned to precedents from nature and science instead. German biologist Ernst Haeckel's book *Kunstformen der Natur* (1904) was a profound influence on many architects and designers. Projects such as Hendrik Petrus Berlage's Jellyfish chandelier, the Paris Métro station entrances by Hector Guimard (figure 01) and many others within the Art Deco and Art Nouveau movements were greatly inspired by it. Much of this so-called nature-inspired architecture emerged continuously from the 1920s until the '60s and '70s, including examples such as Rudolf Steiner's Haus Duldeck (1916), Frederick Kiesler's Endless House (1950) and Eero Saarinen's TWA Terminal (1962). Nature-driven architecture still occurs today, too, with works like Santiago Calatrava's City of Arts and Sciences in Valencia (1998) and Achim Mengese's web-like ICD/ITKE Research Pavilion in Stuttgart (2012). Although each of these projects employed different tools, they all mimicked the intelligent processes of living organisms, translating them into architecture rather than simply using them as inspiration for form and appearance.

Figure 01 (left)
Paris Métro entrance,
by Hector Guimard

Figure 02 (right)
Notre Dame
du Haut Chapel
in Ronchamp,
by Le Corbusier

## Design processes driven by geometry

Geometric rules and proportions have been the main driver for other important architects. Louis Sullivan, one of the most significant architects of the modern movement, used techniques such as quadrature and triangulation to design decorative patterns (Menocal and Twombly 2000), while Frank Lloyd Wright applied geometrical rules and proportions to the design of his Unity Temple in Chicago (1908). Wright's design was based on a 2 metre (7 foot) grid, enhanced with dimensions that derived from quadrature and were not compatible with the grid (Jormakka 2007). Later, Le Corbusier tried to systematize his own proportional design methods in the book *Modulor* (1948), praising the golden section as the gateway to beauty. He also applied his famous Modulor proportional diagram to two of his masterpieces, the Notre Dame du Haut Chapel in Ronchamp (1954; figure 02) and the Philips Pavilion in Brussels (1958). Both are among his most geometrically advanced projects, proving that the Modulor proportion rules could function as a toolbox offering unpredictable outputs.

## Design processes driven by context

Other architects have used their response to the site and the use of morphological and typological elements as their design approach, forming the design movement known as postmodernism. Aldo Rossi, for example, used basic types often common in the historical context of Italian cities (the octagon, colonnade, arch and so on) in very pure shapes, regardless of function or scale. The octagonal tower shape, for instance, was used in his designs for a secondary school in Broni, Italy (1971), as well as the Teatro del Mondo in Venice (1979) and La Conica, the coffee pot he designed for Alessi (1983; Jormakka 2007).

For Oswald Mathias Ungers, responding to the site involved defining common silhouettes and morphological characteristics, such as materiality, texture, arches, symmetry, roofs and angles, then trying to reproduce these in a new composition. His housing complex at Lützowplatz, Berlin (built in 1979 but demolished in 2013) is a typical example of this approach (Ungers 2011). Mario Botta, on the other hand, uses simple, often symmetrical, modernist forms in combination with site-inspired materials, colours and traditional building techniques. His single-family house in Ligornetto, Switzerland (1976), for example, bears the characteristic stripes often found in the region (Cappellato 2004).

## Design processes driven by performance

In contrast to the above, a number of architects and engineers have practised a completely different form-finding method. They have focused on the minimal possible form, deriving from structural performance and material properties. The building's relationship with its context plays only a minor role. Vladimir Shukhov's steel tower, built for an industrial exhibition in Nizhny Novgorod in 1896, was the world's first ever hyperboloid diagrid structure. This structure was then duplicated in much of Shukhov's later work, including the telecommunication tower (Shukhov Tower) that he built in Moscow, which still stands today (figure 03). This structure achieves a perfect combination of mathematical shape, optimized structure and material performance (Khan-Magomedov 1987). Heinz Isler's concrete shell structure for the Wyss Garden Centre in Solothurn, Switzerland, built in 1962, assumes similar hyperboloid shapes, covering a span of 650 square meters (7,000 square feet), with a shell thickness of just 60 mm (2½ inches) (Chilton 2000). Finally, Frei Otto, investigating tensile membrane structures, developed the Munich Olympic Stadium in 1972 (figure 04) – a definite highlight of his career (Otto and Rasch 1996). Although developed at a time when computers where not used in architecture at all, the design approach adopted by Shukhov, Isler and Otto is strongly linked to contemporary performative design techniques.

Figure 03 (left)
Diagrid on Shukhov
Tower in Moscow,
by Vladimir Shukhov

Figure 04 (right)
Munich Olympic
Stadium, by Frei Otto
and Günther Behnisch

# 1.2 / GENERATIVE FORM-FINDING PROCESSES

So what is 'generative design' exactly? There is no single definition of the term, but many complementary definitions with common characteristics, which vary according to different architectural theorists. Overall it can be described as a design method where generation of form is based on rules or algorithms, often deriving from computational tools, such as Processing, Rhinoceros, Grasshopper and other scripting platforms. During the late 1980s and early '90s, just before the boom of computational architecture, Peter Eisenman started applying a set of design techniques, such as scaling, fractals, overlay and superposition, influenced by Jacques Derrida's Deconstruction theory. Eisenman applied these techniques in relation to rules of order, developing several projects on this basis, such as the Biocentrum in Frankfurt (1987) and the Nunotani Corporation headquarters in Tokyo (1992; figure 05) (Eisenman 2004). One could claim that his design method was the first contemporary generative design attempt. As software started to offer new possibilities, Eisenman introduced other techniques to his approach, such as morphing images, which was soon followed by UNstudio and their concept of the 'Manimal', a computer-generated icon that merges a lion, snake and human to represent the hybrid building (Van Berkel and Bos 1999).

The technique of folding appeared in Eisenman's Rebstockbad in 1991 (Eisenman 2004) and, as computational tools advanced further, Greg Lynn started applying new tools such as animation, splines, NURBS (non-uniform rational basis splines) and isomorphic polysurfaces, influencing a whole wave of architectural production, often described as 'blob architecture' (Lynn 1999). As algorithms and scripting become more accessible to architects and designers, and digital fabrication more affordable, parametric and panelization tools, simulation software, optimization and generative algorithms are dominating generative design techniques.

Figure 05
Nunotani Corporation headquarters in Tokyo, by Peter Eisenman

In their book *Generative Gestaltung* (Lazzeroni, Bohnacker, Groß and Laub 2009), the authors define generative design as a cyclical process based on a simple abstracted idea, which is applied to a rule or algorithm (figure 06). It then translates into a source code, which produces serial output via a computer. The outputs return through a feedback loop, enabling the designer to reinform the algorithm and the source code. It is an iterative operation, relying on the feedback exchange between the designer and the design system.

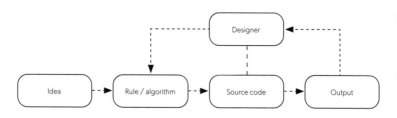

Celestino Soddu (1994) defines generative design as 'a morphogenetic process using algorithms structured as nonlinear systems for endless unique and unrepeatable results performed by an idea-code, as in nature'. Indeed, the notions of generative design and digital morphogenesis are strongly associated. The term 'morphogenesis' derives from the Greek words *morphe* (μορφή, meaning 'form') and *genesis* (γένεσις, meaning 'birth'), so could be literally translated as 'birth of form'. As with the term 'generative design', there is no unique definition for morphogenesis, and it seems that the terminology is changing in relation to emerging technologies and techniques.

Branko Kolarevic (2003) describes digital morphogenesis as follows: 'The predictable relationships between design

Figure 06
Generative design
process diagram,
by Lazzeroni, Bohnacker,
Groß and Laub

and representations are abandoned in favour of computationally generated complexities. Models of design capable of consistent, continual and dynamic transformation are replacing the static norms of conventional processes. Complex curvilinear geometries are produced with the same ease as Euclidean geometries of planar shapes and cylindrical, spherical or conical forms. The plan no longer "generates" the design; sections attain a purely analytical role. Grids, repetitions and symmetries lose their past raison d'être, as infinite variability becomes as feasible as modularity, and as mass-customization presents alternatives to mass-production.' In addition, he sees such methods as unpredictable mechanisms of creation, relying on digital tools, where traditional architectural values are replaced by complexity, asymmetry, curvilinearity, infinite variability and mass customization. Architectural morphology is focusing on the emergent and adaptable qualities of form. Form is no longer being made, but found, based on a set of rules or algorithms, in association with mainly digital, but also physical, tools and techniques. They imply the rules; the entire process follows.

Michael Hensel describes digital morphogenesis as a 'self-organization process, underlying the growth of living organisms, from which architects can learn' (Hensel, Menges and Weinstock 2006). In their latest book, Rivka and Robert Oxman (2013) categorize form generation into six dominant models in relation to its main driver: mathematical, tectonic, material, natural, fabricational and performative. They see digital morphogenesis as 'the exploitation of generative media for the derivation of material form and its evolutionary mutation'. Its key concepts include topological geometries, genetic algorithms, parametric design and performance analysis.

Finally, Toyo Ito compares 'generative order' to the growth mechanism of trees, whose form derives from the repetition of simple rules, creating a very complex order (Turnbull 2012). A tree's shape responds to its surroundings, blurring the boundaries of interior and exterior spaces – qualities that are easy to recognize in Ito's Serpentine Gallery Pavilion in London (2002; figure 07).

Figure 07
Serpentine Gallery
Pavilion in London,
by Toyo Ito

# 1.3 / THE APPROACH OF THIS BOOK

This book presents a series of undergraduate student projects that emerged from Studio 04, a research-led design unit headed by the author at the University of Liverpool's School of Architecture. A modified generative method was applied to each of these projects in order to assess its potential for developing innovative architectural solutions, incorporating contextual, performative, structural, material and typological parameters. The programme was also designed to satisfy learning outcomes specified by the Royal Institute of British Architects for an accredited Part 1 degree in architecture. The form-generation method applied was based on three main phases – Analysis, Morphogenesis and Metamorphosis (figure 08) – with the aim of producing complete architectural proposals in an educational framework. This was a non-linear design approach, operating as a continuous loop, which allowed all design phases to reinform each other.

Figure 08
Generative
design method,
by Asterios Agkathidis

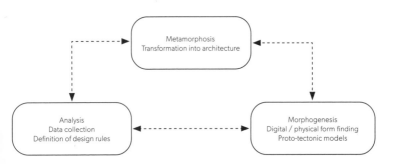

Metamorphosis
Transformation into architecture

Analysis
Data collection
Definition of design rules

Morphogenesis
Digital / physical form finding
Proto-tectonic models

Analysis focused on data collection for various aspects, such as context, programme, material, structure and performance. Morphogenesis, digital or physical, then targeted the generation of abstract prototypes, based on spatial and organizational principles, including unit accumulation, surface continuity, faceting, volume deformation or subtraction, and algorithmic patterning. After undergoing a phase of iterations, the resultant not-to-scale 'proto-tectonic' structures (Frampton 2001) were then 'transformed' into building proposals, including floor plans, sections and elevations, as well as physical and digital models and all their derivatives (atmospheric images, visualizations, etc.). The metamorphosis of an abstract prototype into a building proposal could occur in two different ways. It could either be literal (a direct transformation into a building envelope and structure) or operational (functioning as an apparatus, which could generate design solutions in various scales and arrangements).

The design studio unit consisted of 60 students (part of a cohort of 240 in that year), tutored by five tutors, and the programme took place within a 12-week semester. Students worked collaboratively for the first four weeks (Analysis and Morphogenesis) and developed their individual projects during the remaining eight. Final submissions were then marked by all studio tutors, and moderated and tested by external examiners. The students had never followed a design approach like this before, and had to be trained in computer-based design techniques during the semester. They were encouraged to use both physical and digital techniques, and to use their findings from one to inform processes in the other. Surveys were also conducted in order to gauge student opinion. The whole programme aimed to answer the following questions:

- How can generative design methodology be integrated in an undergraduate design studio module?

- What are its strengths and weaknesses?

- Does the applied design methodology produce innovative design solutions, and does it enhance students' design skills and future employability?

- Does the integration of generative design methodology at undergraduate level seem appropriate?

In combination with the preceding pages' discussion of generative design techniques and their implementation in architecture, the projects selected for this book offer a useful collection of illustrated design studies. Together they present a handbook of ideas, suitable as both an educational textbook and an inspirational research handbook for design scholars and practitioners.

# CONTINUOUS
# SURFACES

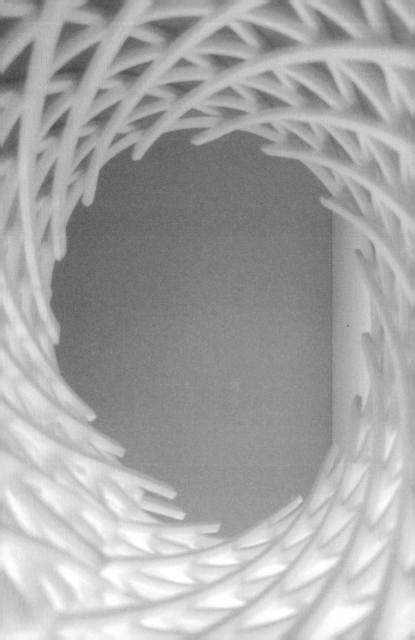

# 2.1 / SOFT MESH

Analysis: Properties of curved timber in relation to variable spatial qualities, such as high and low, wide and narrow, open and enclosed; precedent studies of Shigeru Ban's Centre Pompidou-Metz.

Morphogenesis: This project developed out of exploration with a bendable timber mesh and its material properties. It was constructed as a plain surface made from linear elements, exploring different weaving techniques in relation to the geometries and spatial typologies they were able to host (see pages 26–27). Physical working models were constructed out of balsa wood and foam board, generating a set of iterations. Digital models followed, exploring the possibilities offered by NURBS as design surfaces.

Metamorphosis: As a second step, contextual, structural and programmatic parameters were defined and applied to the design process. The proposal was for a food market hall in a dense urban context. It evolved as a continuous timber mesh structure, covered with PTFE foil, defining both roof and columns (see pages 28–29) and allowing a smooth transition between indoor and outdoor spaces. The switch from physical to digital models was essential in order to control the geometry of the roof structure.

Design study
by Jianxuan Chen

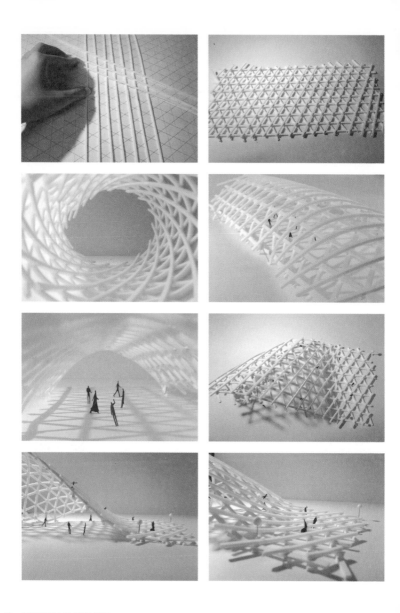

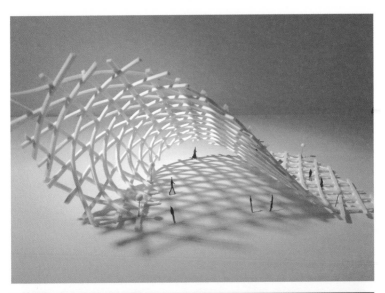

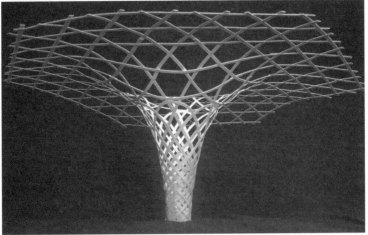

Structural–spatial iterations
of the timber mesh surface

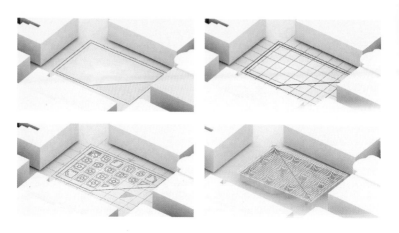

Site analysis and design parameter definition

Left: Interior view
of the market hall

Below: Longitudinal
section through the
canopy structure

# 2.2 / DOUBLE-CURVED SHELLS

Analysis: Concrete shells; precedent studies of Félix Candela's Lomas de Cuernavaca Chapel and Toyo Ito's Kakamigahara Crematorium.

Morphogenesis: This project investigated concrete shell primitives and their structural performance. Simple, primitive shapes were first modelled and analysed (see pages 32–33), then combined in large-scale continuous surfaces, exploring regular and irregular iterations, as well as different degrees of curvature.

Metamorphosis: Site and programmatic parameters were used to define the footprint of the intended design – a market hall – preserving the existing trees on the site. The final roof proposal constituted a double-curved surface, covering a floor plan that was based on a Voronoi pattern. The concrete roof–column shell structure was perforated with a circular pattern to allow variable lighting conditions in the market hall's interior spaces (see page 35).

Design study by
Xu Chen, Yuhui Qi,
Peiyu Yang, Ruinan
Zhang and Yuan Zhai

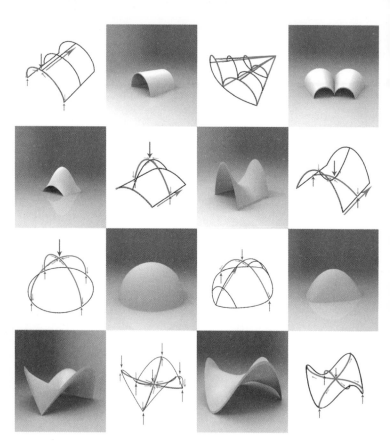

Iterations of concrete shell
primitives, in relation to forces
of tension and compression

Accumulation of shell units
into continuous surfaces

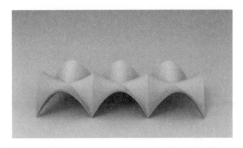

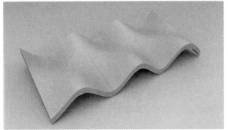

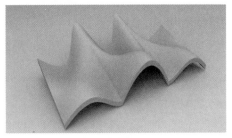

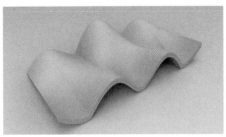

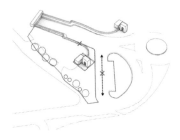

The site's two parts are unified

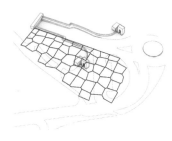

A Voronoi grid is applied to the site

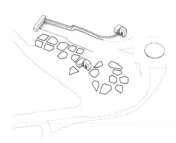

The Voronoi grid forms circulation and plan organization

Areas occupied by the schedule of accommodation

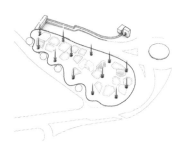

Position of columns is determined

Canopy structure emerges

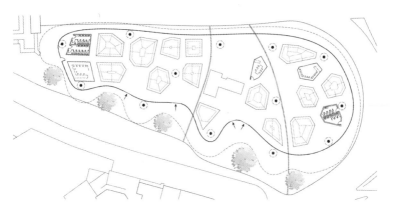

Floor plan

Interior view

Exterior view

# 2.3 / HYPER PARABOLOIDS

Analysis: Paraboloid steel structures; precedent studies of Vladimir Shukhov's telecommunication tower.

Morphogenesis: This project evolved as a continuous hyper paraboloid surface, which derived from joining an array of inverted polygonal profiles of 'hills and valleys'. The resultant double-curved surface was constructed from planar linear beams. Iterations of the inverted hill-and-valley system, in relation to span and angle of the polyline, were explored in various prototypes (see pages 40–43).

Metamorphosis: In this case, the translation from prototype to architecture was almost literal. Iterations of span, beam thickness and height in relation to programme, scale and context were adjusted and optimized for the site – the extension of a historical harbourside building in order to shelter a ferry terminal, with retail and gastronomic facilities (see pages 44–45). The proposed roofscape evolved out of the roof of the existing building. It stretches as a lace surface above the threshold between the square and the floating platform, providing the terminal's interiors with optimum daylight conditions.

Design study by
Jinglei Fu, Xiao Qi,
Aqsa Imtiaz, Nadezda
Kazakova, Xuerui Lu
and Amy Whitmore

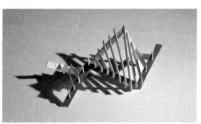

Double-curved surface iterative models

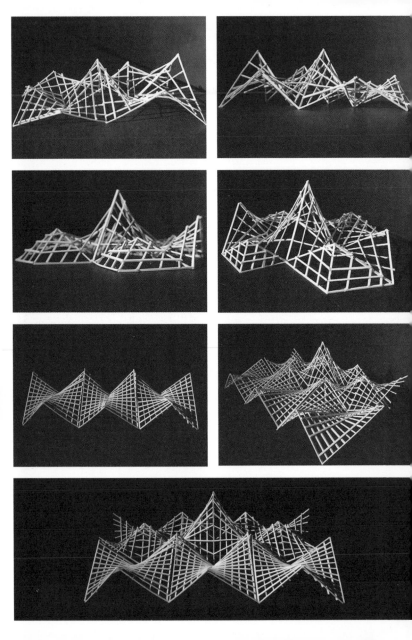

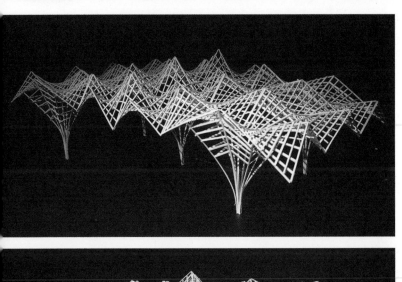

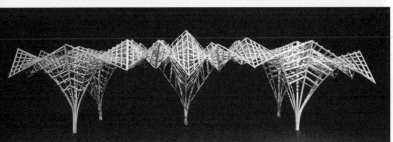

Iterations in span and mesh density,
and arrangement of double-curved
surface models

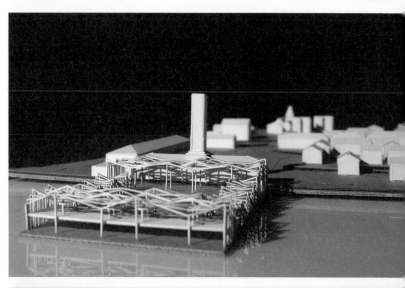

Ferry terminal arrangement in context

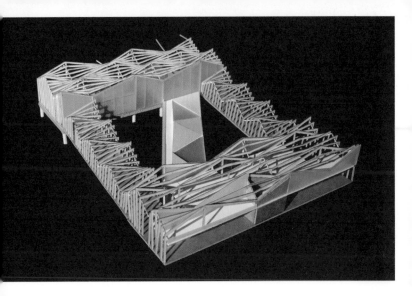

Perspective view

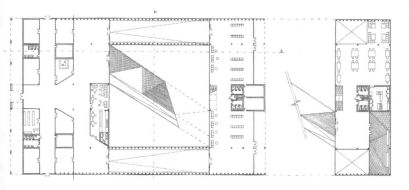

Floor plan

# MODULARITY
# AND ACCUMULATION

# 3.1 / INTERLOCKING UNITS

Analysis: Modular accumulation of space units; precedent studies of Le Corbusier's Unité d'Habitation and Charles Correa's Kanchanjunga apartment tower.

Morphogenesis: This series of prototypes derived from a rectangular block, which formed units in various combinations (see page 50). These enabled the design of various clusters, which aimed for balanced layouts of void and solid, interior and exterior, covered and uncovered space, orientation and height (see pages 51–53). The cluster prototypes offered an almost infinite number of iterations.

Metamorphosis: The size of the units was modified to accommodate one-, two- or three-bedroom apartments, and the building envelope was created to respond to the conditions of the site, embedding parameters such as optimal circulation, lighting and ventilation, as well as a harmonious relationship between public and private zones (see page 54). The final building proposal was developed around a courtyard typology, offering a variety of single- or double-height spaces and generous outdoor areas. Despite the simple, toolbox-based generative system, the final output achieves a high degree of complexity.

Design study by
Xiao Gu, Yuedi Liu,
Yangting Yang, Jinglei Fu
and Wenxuan Zhang

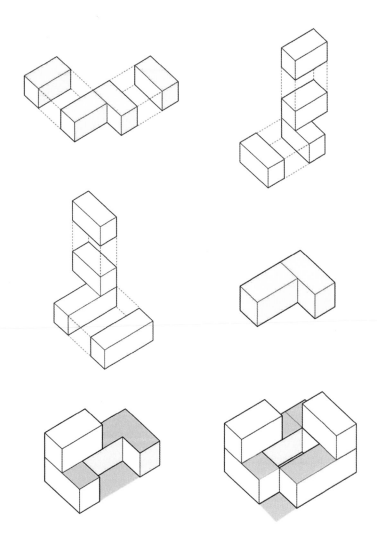

Unit formation diagrams

Cluster formation of modular
unit iterations

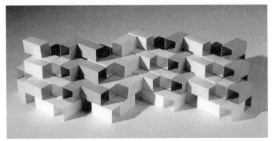
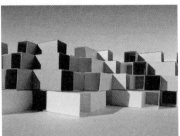
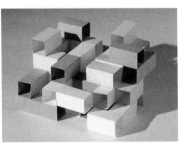
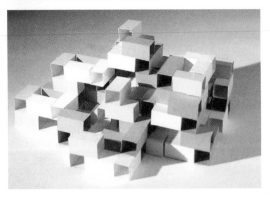

Cluster formation: iterative models

Massing is adjusted around the courtyard

Rear side is adjusted to natural light conditions

Units are adjusted into massing

Circulation and community spaces are embedded

Transparent and opaque areas are defined

Building's height is adjusted to the context

Building's access is arranged according to privacy levels

Public

Private

Main Street

Green areas are distributed on terraces and roofs

Building openings are matched to functions

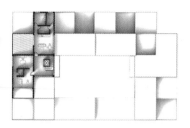

Seventh floor

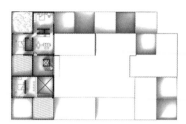

Sixth floor

Fifth floor

Fourth floor

Third floor

Second floor

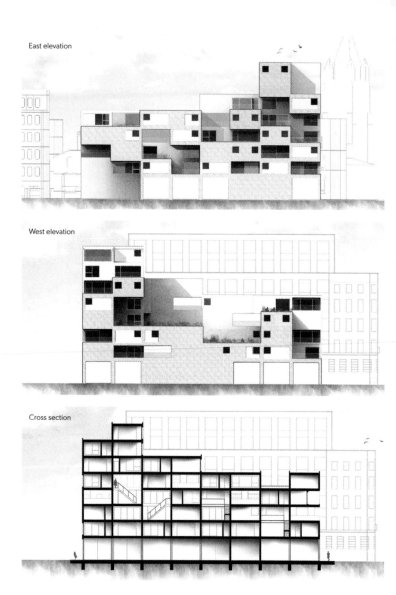

East elevation

West elevation

Cross section

Perspective exterior view

# 3.2 / IRREGULAR UNITS

Analysis: Accumulation of irregular units; precedent studies of Kisho Kurokawa's Metabolist projects.

Morphogenesis: This design study evolved as a set of units that were irregular in layout and height. They were assembled on a vertical shelving system and a horizontal grid, which defined slabs and enclosed space. Clusters were composed according to spatial criteria, such as relationships between solid and void, open and enclosed, indoor and outdoor. The generative system allowed a vast number of iterations to emerge, all of which offered a high degree of plasticity and a range of spatial qualities (see pages 60–63).

Metamorphosis: The building developed in response to its context, in terms of circulatory, programmatic and typological requirements (see page 64). However, in contrast to the other design studies in this book, this project adopted mainly the prototype's design logic, rather than its form. The different apartment types were developed with the addition of bedrooms, living/dining areas and services units (see page 65). These in turn operated as modules, accumulated within a predetermined massing that was then remodelled to offer spacious public areas. A similar method was used to design the building's facade. A modular system evolved along a structural grid, and various cladding materials (e.g., glass, opaque panels and photovoltaic cells) were distributed along the east, west and south elevations (see pages 66–67). The final proposal is a residential apartment block, including two storeys of retail and a rooftop restaurant.

Design study by
Charlotte Brookshouse,
Shimou Chen,
James Crookston,
Minhui Huang,
Lazaros Kyratsous,
Longfei Wang,
Nan Yang and Yuan Zhai

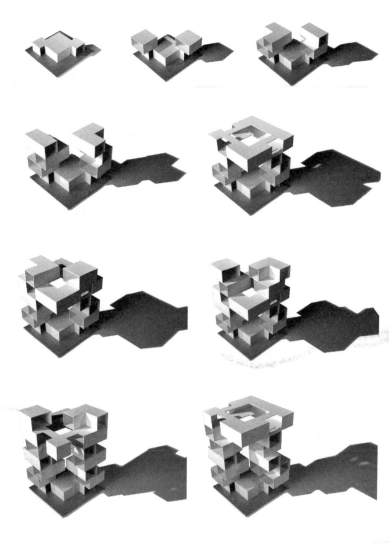

Shelving system: iterative models

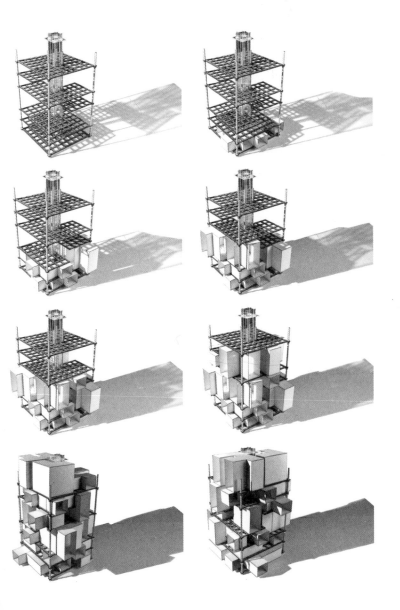

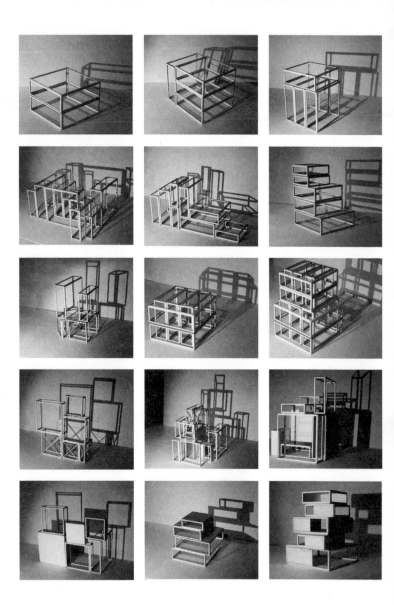

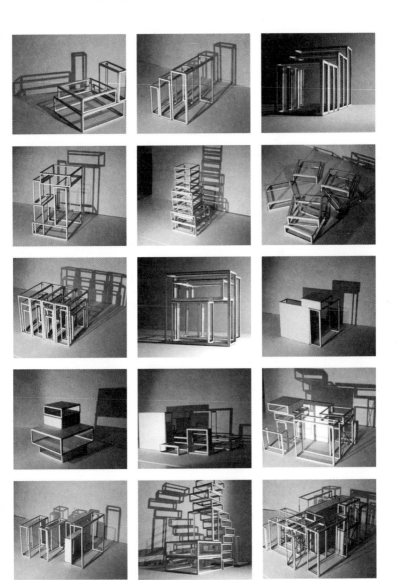

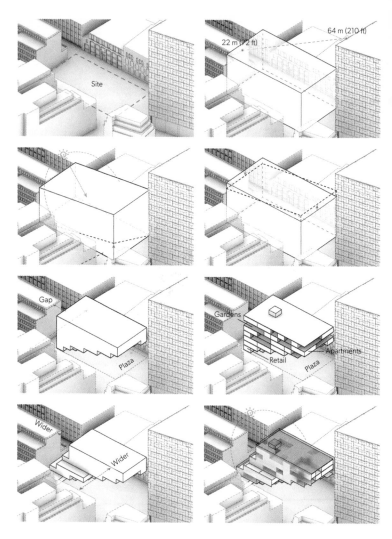

Massing evolves as a set
of contextual, programmatic
and environmental parameters

Composition of apartment units

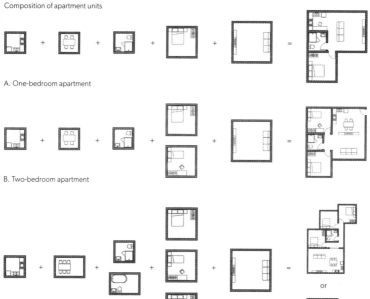

A. One-bedroom apartment

B. Two-bedroom apartment

C. Three-bedroom apartment,
   two options

or

Typical floor plan

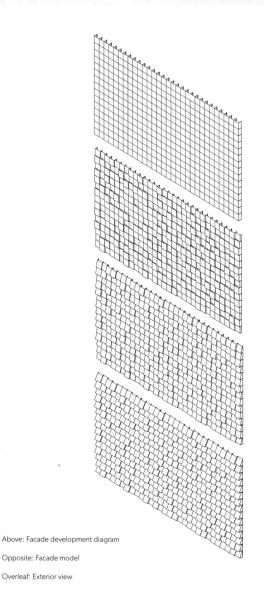

Above: Facade development diagram

Opposite: Facade model

Overleaf: Exterior view

# DEFORMATION
# AND SUBTRACTION

# 4.1 / TWISTED BLOCK

Analysis: Load-bearing stone structures; precedent studies of Wandel Hoefer Lorch & Hirsch's New Synagogue, Dresden.

Morphogenesis: This project evolved as a twisted rectangular volume, examining the application of both physical and digital twisting techniques. Physical twisting was achieved by applying gradual pressure to timber frames arranged around an axis (see page 74). Digital twisting was applied to a block, which was then contoured, laser-cut and assembled (see page 75). By introducing small gaps in the timber frames, various lighting possibilities were explored.

Metamorphosis: The design proposal was to offer shelter to a market hall neighbouring a busy traffic junction. After analysing the site and the required schedule of accommodation, the twisting technique was applied digitally to an initial 3D massing model. The final building envelope was then deformed to the degree required by its integration into the site. The market hall offers spectacular interior spaces as well as usable terraced exterior areas (see pages 76–79). It is a load-bearing, stone structural skin, reinforced with a steel frame.

Design study by Sean
Bailey and David Barker

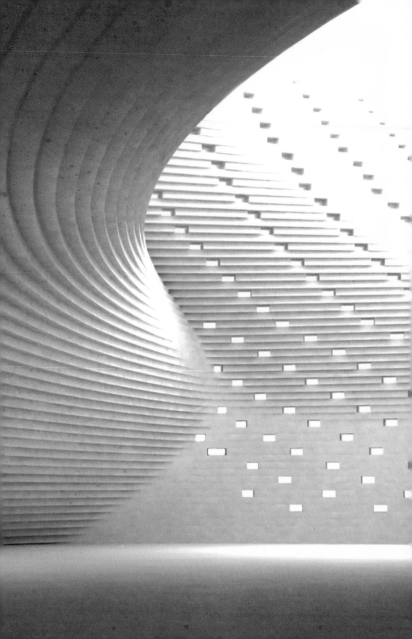

Twisted volume
iterations

Digitally produced twisted models,
materialized using laser-cut MDF frames

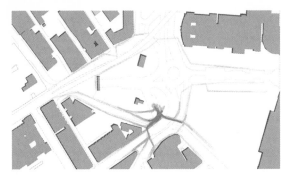

Defining circulation paths and access

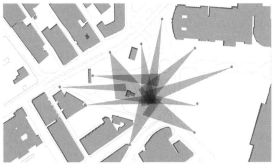

Defining views to the building

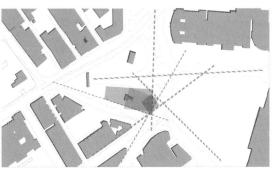

Aligning massing to the site

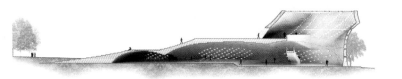

Longitudinal section

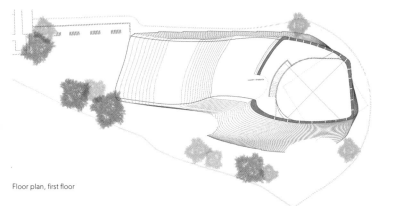

Floor plan, first floor

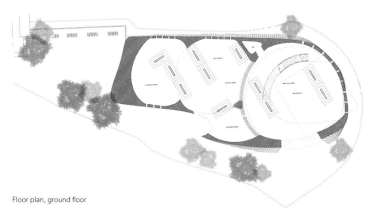

Floor plan, ground floor

Interior view

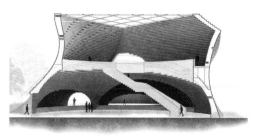

Cross section

# 4.2 / POROUS SPACE

Analysis: Concrete casting and its properties; precedent studies of Frederick Kiesler's Endless House and Eero Saarinen's TWA Terminal.

Morphogenesis: This design study explored the notion of a porous space, inspired in particular by Kiesler's Endless House. It was a formal exploration using both physical and digital modelling tools. Balloons in three different sizes, filled with water, were used as forms for the plaster-casting stage. After the plaster had dried out and the balloons had been removed, a porous, 'Swiss cheese'-like structure remained (see pages 82–83). As a second step, the structure was analysed and then remodelled in a digital environment, using Rhinoceros and the T-Splines plug-in. The final output was a 3D-printed physical model (see pages 84–85).

Metamorphosis: This design was intended to host a market hall, including areas dedicated to gastronomy as well as public leisure spaces, located in a central urban environment. The building developed in response to issues of context, circulation, programme and typology discovered during development (see pages 86–87). It takes the form of a concrete structural shell, which allows the option of roof lights, and entrance and window openings. It embraces leisure zones and public outdoor areas, while also transforming the space from roof to wall and floor (see pages 88–89).

Design study by
Nojan Adami, Yiqiang
Zhao and Zhenyu Zhu

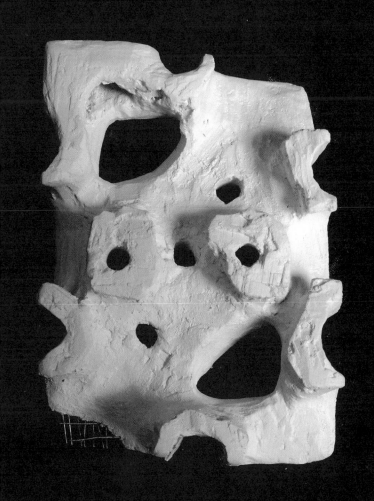

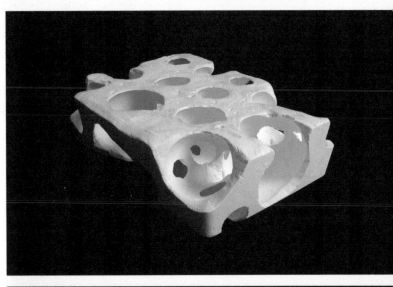

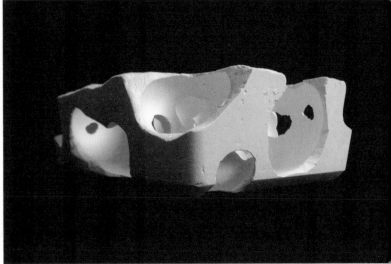

Porous shell: handmade plaster model

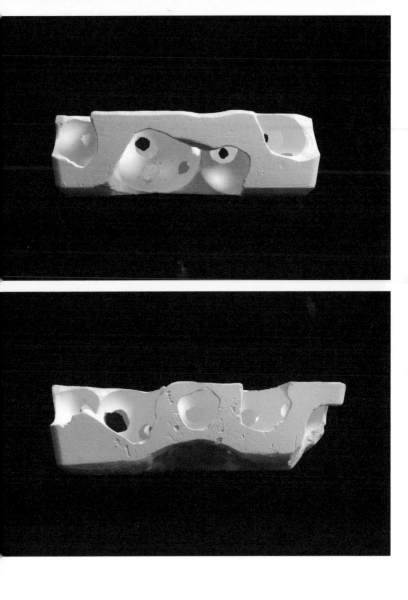

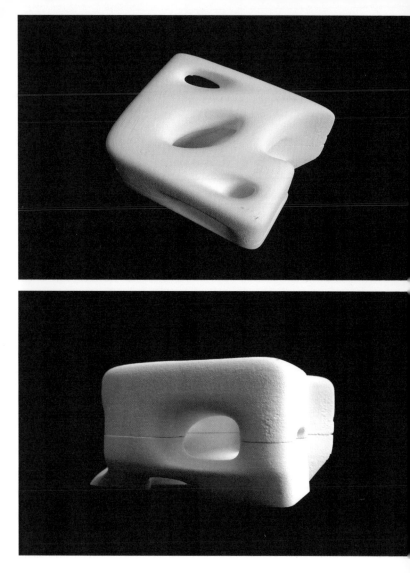

Porous shell: 3D-printed model

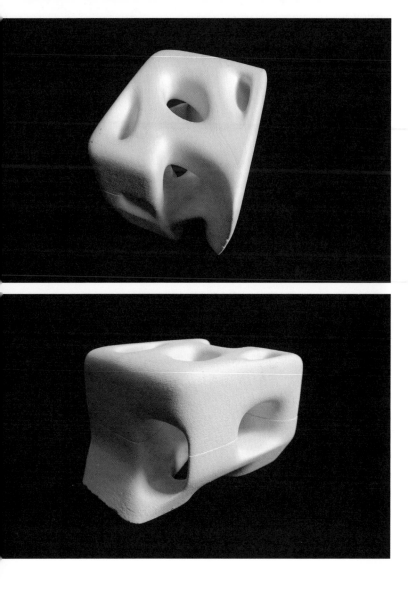

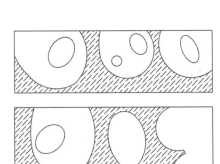

Left: Sectional diagrams of physical and digital models

Below: Forming the building's footprint from the circulation diagram and programmatic requirements

Bottom: Adjusting the massing to its context

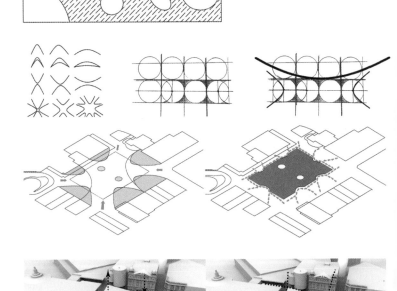

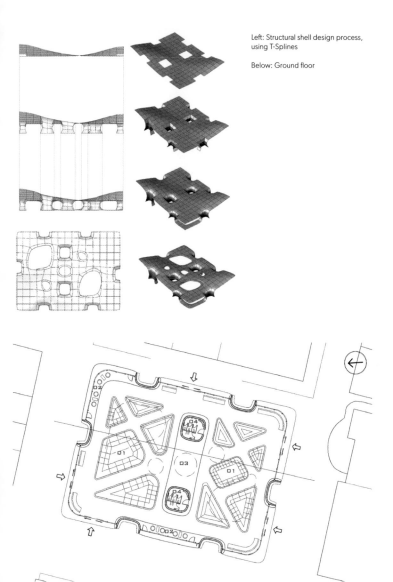

Left: Structural shell design process, using T-Splines

Below: Ground floor

# ALGORITHMIC
# PATTERNS

# 5.1 / TESSELLATED PLANES

Analysis: Steel structures; precedent studies of Toyo Ito's Serpentine Gallery Pavilion.

Morphogenesis: This project investigated three generative algorithms, using Rhinoceros 5 and Grasshopper, in search of possible structural patterns. The first pattern was based on attractor points and grid deformation, the second explored weaving patterns and techniques, while the third explored irregular tessellation of planar planes (see pages 94–95). After examining iterative models of all three algorithms, the last was chosen for further development.

Metamorphosis: The footprint and massing of this central market hall was derived from contextual parameters, such as alignment with street views, and the heights and axes of neighbouring structures. The roof was then formed in various directions in order to allow views to the prestigious buildings around the site, such as a library and a train station. Finally, the tessellation algorithm was applied to the roof, defining the building structural system and envelope (see pages 96–97). As well as providing glazing, the aluminium panels give the hall a unique appearance (see pages 98–99).

Design study
by Nojan Adami

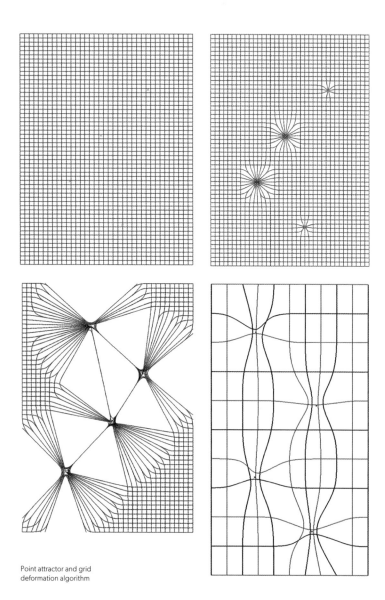

Point attractor and grid
deformation algorithm

Left: Weaving algorithm

Below: Tessellation algorithm

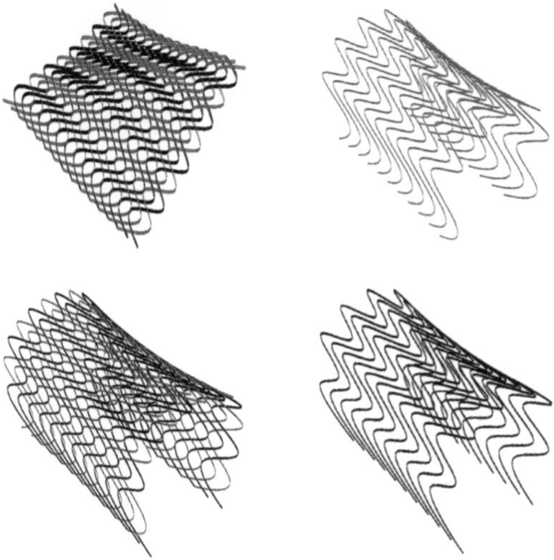

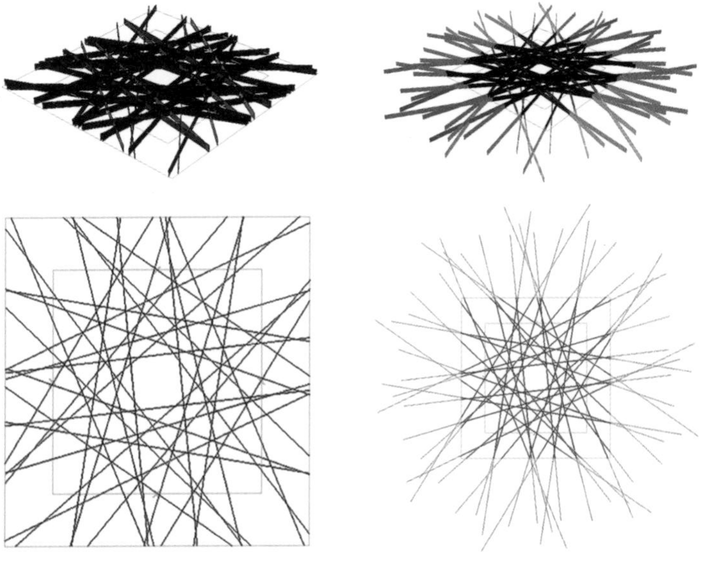

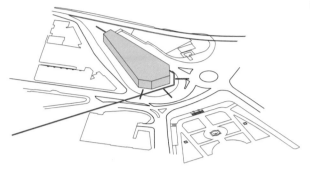

Solar path analysis

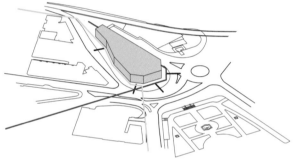

Building massing
and main circulation
axis on site

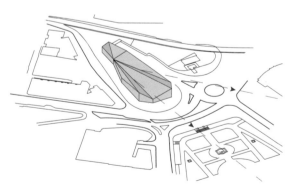

Building's roof
is adjusted to
accommodate views

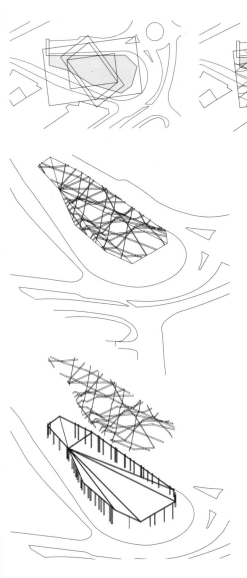

Tessellation algorithm is applied to building envelope

Street view

Aerial view

# 5.2 / VORONOI SURFACE

Analysis: Timber frame structures; precedent studies of Barkow Leibinger's Campus Restaurant.

Morphogenesis: This project experimented with a Voronoi pattern algorithm. For the first stage it used physical models to assess configurations of different shapes and sizes, as well as various degrees of extrusion (see pages 102–3). At the next stage it shifted to digital modelling, examining the Voronoi pattern parametrization and its application to three-dimensional and double-curved geometries (see pages 104–7).

Metamorphosis: This design was intended to provide shelter for a ferry terminal, incorporating retail and cultural spaces. During the final stage the Voronoi algorithm was applied to the site (see page 108), defining the main areas of accommodation as well as the position of the columns, and the landscape design of the neighbouring square. The final roof proposal is an irregular vault structure, with its laminated timber frame covered by PTFE foil, allowing continuity of natural light as well as variable degrees of transparency (see pages 112–13).

Design study by Liang Gao, Yiwei Gao, Man Jia, Jingchang Li, Xiao Lu and Yihan Zhang

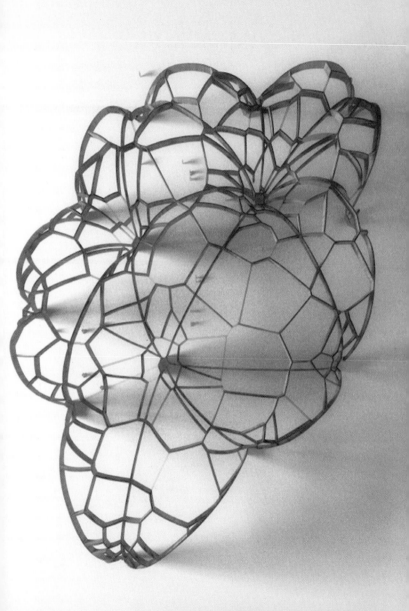

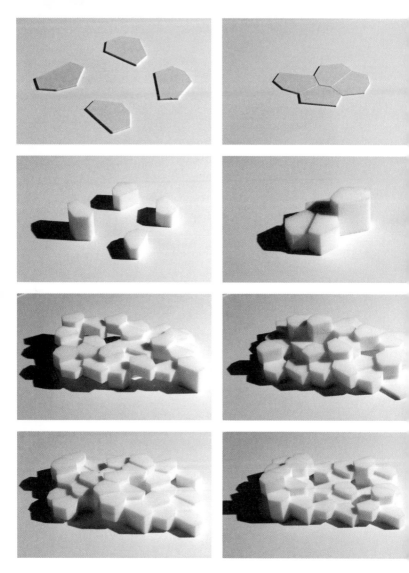

Cluster models, Voronoi blocks

Voronoi pattern applied to rectangular
planes and faceted surfaces

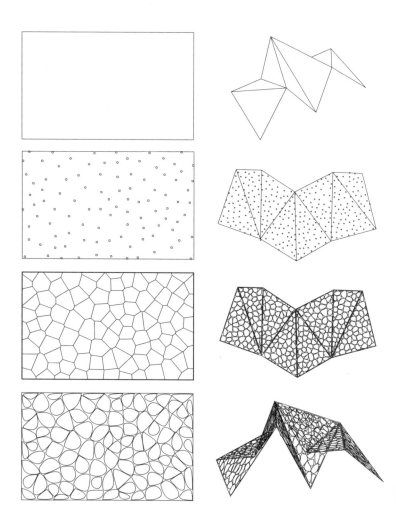

Voronoi pattern applied to
double-curved surfaces

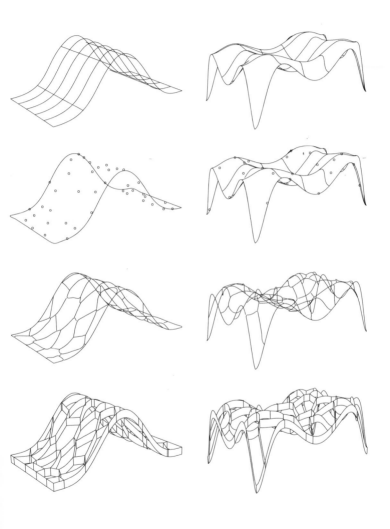

Voronoi pattern applied to solid blocks

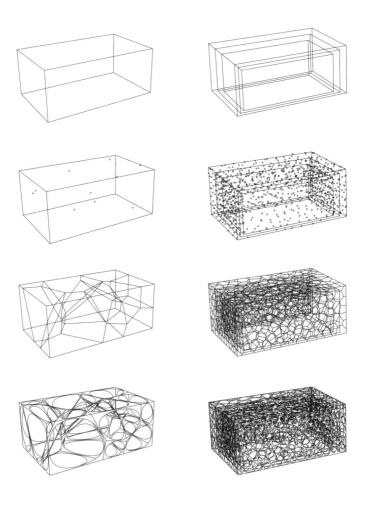

Voronoi pattern applied to paraboloid
and vault surfaces

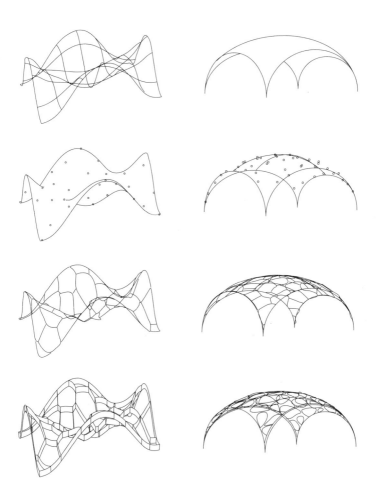

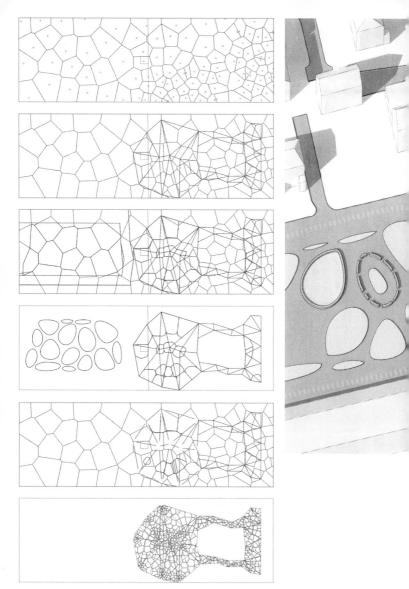

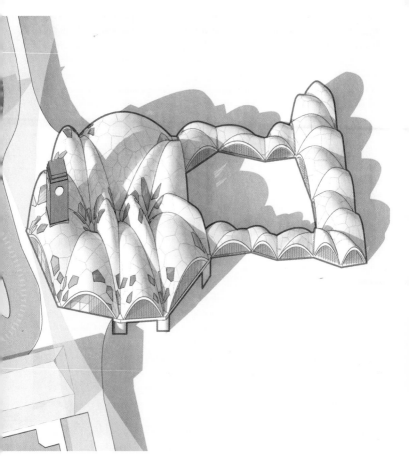

Left: Voronoi algorithm applied
to the building site

Above: Ferry terminal 3D model
in context

Below: Exploded axonometric drawing, demonstrating structure, skin and layout

Opposite: Floor plan

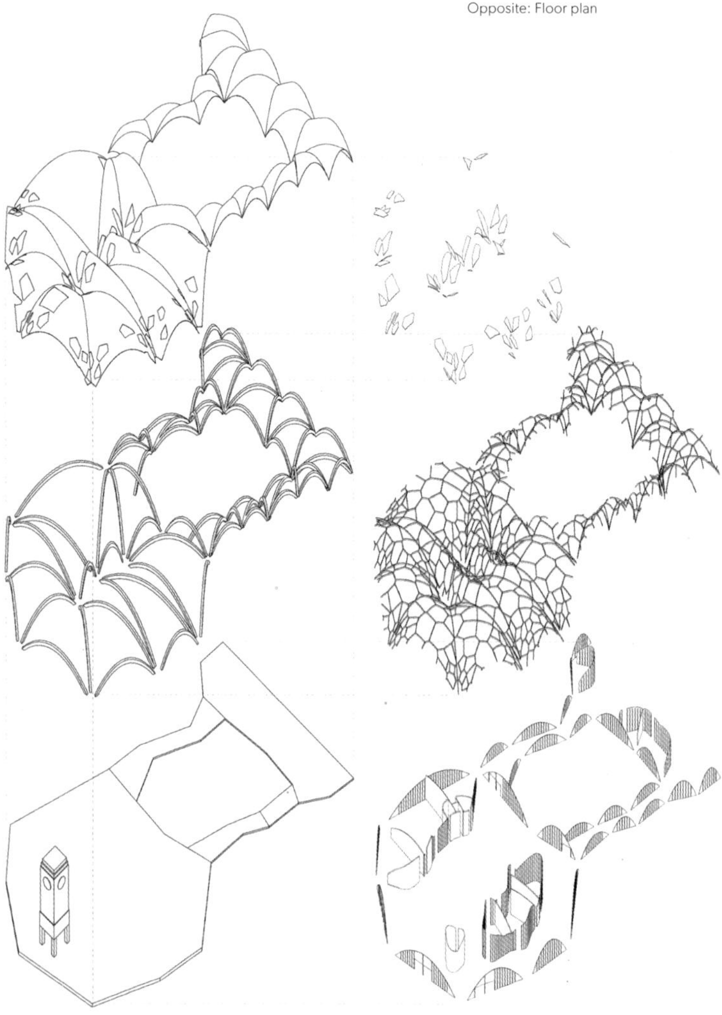

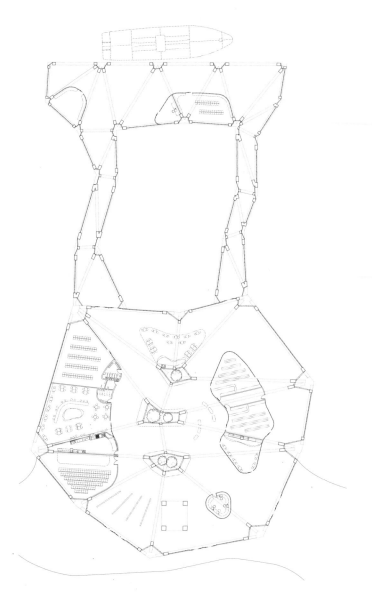

Interior view

Exterior view

# TRIANGULATION

# 6.1 / 3D PENROSE PATTERN

Analysis: Steel frame structures and Penrose tiling.

Morphogenesis: This project employed a generative system comprising two different triangles and five joints (see page 120), inspired by the pattern of Penrose tiling. The combination of triangular components and joint types predetermined geometrical growth in three directions, allowing various spatial conditions to occur (e.g., hills and valleys, enclosures and surfaces). Variable opening types in relation to the heights of enclosed spaces were applied as an additional parameter, which allowed variable lighting conditions to occur.

Metamorphosis: As a second step, contextual, structural and programmatic parameters were applied to the emerging geometry. This was transformed into an envelope capable of having its footprint, height, section, structure, materiality and floor plan adjusted in order to accommodate a market hall in an urban square. Its irregular footprint allowed views to pathways around the building, while also directing visitors to usable outdoor spaces (see pages 122–23).

Design study by Yuedi Liu and Yaoting Yang

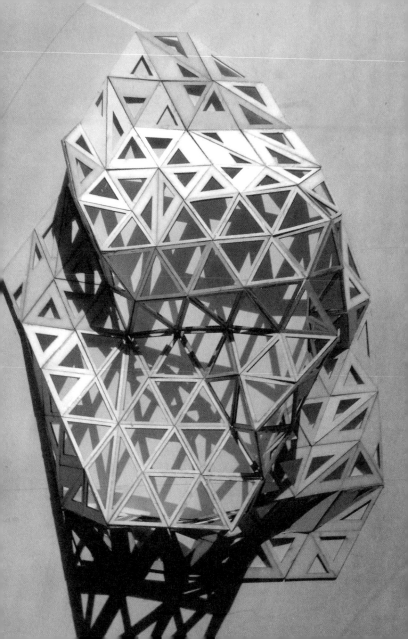

Generative system components:
two main units, five different joints

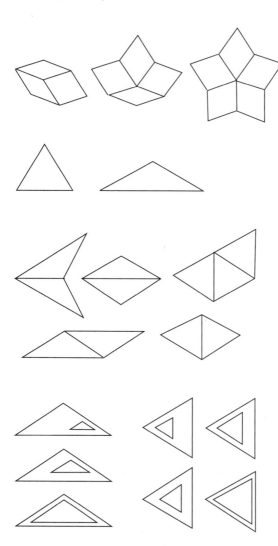

A. Typical Penrose
tiling arrangements

B. The two main
triangle components

C. Five different
joint options

D. Seven different types
of perforation

Morphogenesis: iterations of the
generative system exploring different
spatial conditions in relation
to illumination intensity

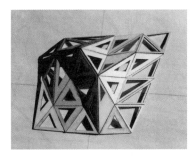

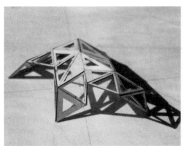

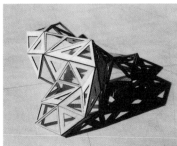

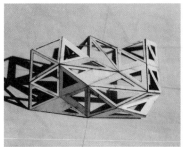

Metamorphosis: adjusting geometry
to structural, programmatic
and contextual parameters

A. Introducing main and secondary
   circulation paths

B. Defining the entrances according
   to neighbouring functions

C. Defining the footprint in order
   to create usable public space
   and channel visitors' views

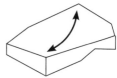

D. The building envelope is adjusted to the site

E. Geometry is translated into structure

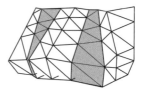

F. Opaque and transparent materials are linked to different public and private zones

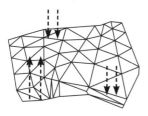

G. The building envelope's height is adjusted to those of neighbouring buildings

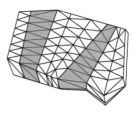

H. The building envelope is adjusted to programmatic requirements

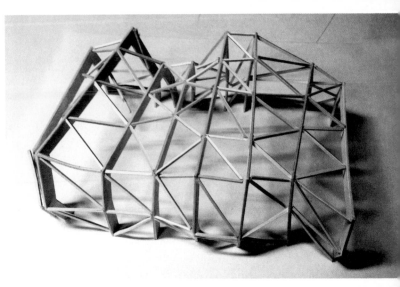

Massing model options in relation to context

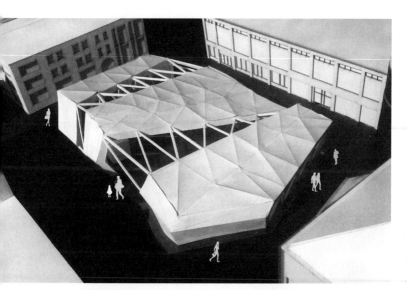

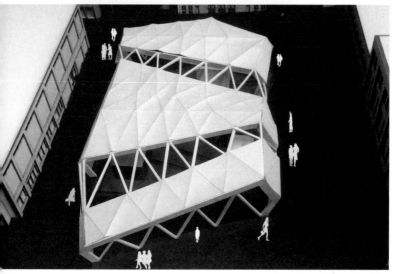

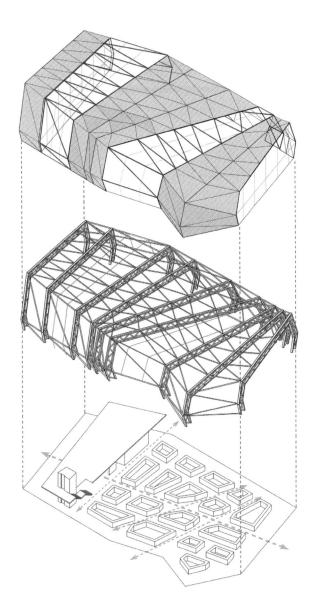

Opposite: Exploded axonometric –
skin, structure and organization

Right: Perspective view

Below: Floor plan, ground floor

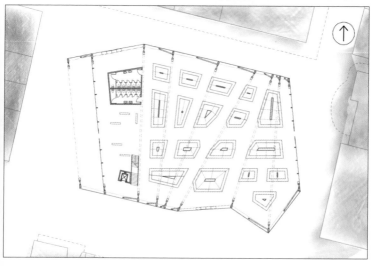

# 6.2 / FACETED LOFT

Analysis: Origami folding techniques; precedent studies of Sancho-Madridejos Architecture Office's Almadanejos Chapel.

Morphogenesis: The generative system used for this project was composed using three different rectangular profiles, which were joined to create a faceted, 'lofted' surface. By modifying each profile's size and vertical arrangement, a set of iteration studies arose, exploring triangulated skin geometry, massing options and tectonics (see pages 130–39).

Metamorphosis: All the geometrical iterations explored in the first phase were then embedded in the design of an apartment block in the centre of Liverpool. Faceted, prismatic geometries shaped the block's massing, which was designed to provide optimal daylight conditions for all of the apartment units (see pages 140–41). In addition, faceted geometries were used to define the block's roofscape and associate it with its urban context. Finally, the building's envelope was transformed into a faceted skin, with extrusions or intrusions that enabled it to accommodate outdoor activities and terraces (see pages 142–43).

Design study by
Yunxia Dai, Emily Gayer,
Tobi Griffiths, Michael
Hill, Haochen Jia, Sen Lin
and Jinhui Zhu

Faceted, lofted surface iterations

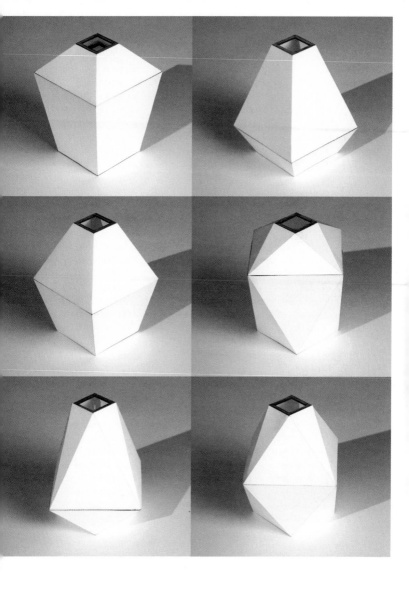

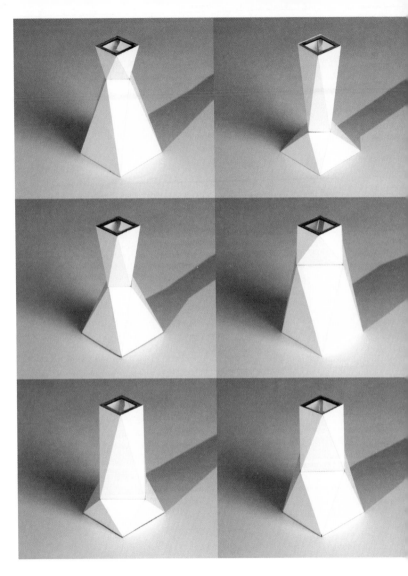

Faceted, lofted surface iterations

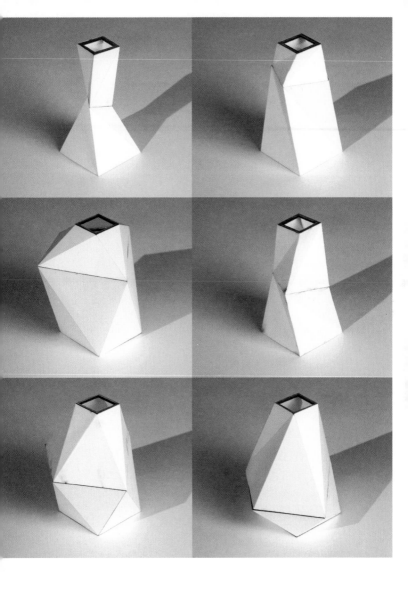

Deformed box iterations

Deformed box iterations

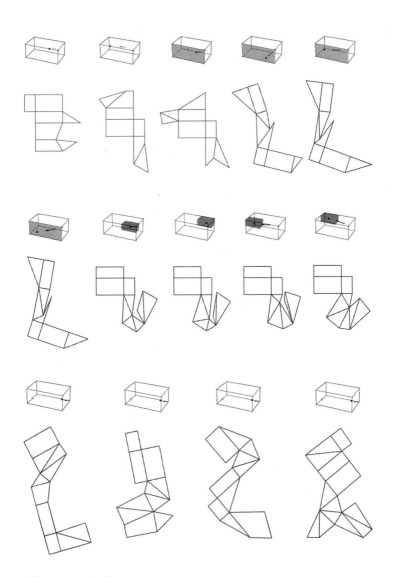

Unfolded triangulated iterative models

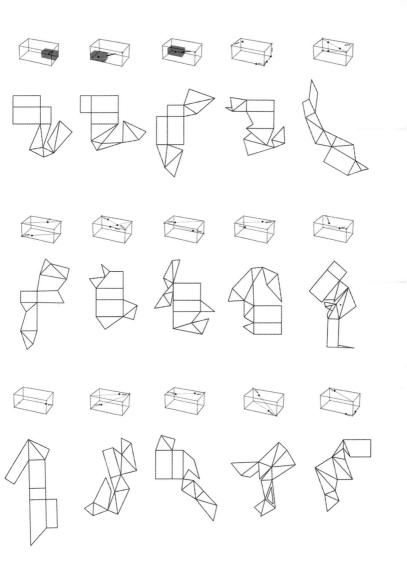

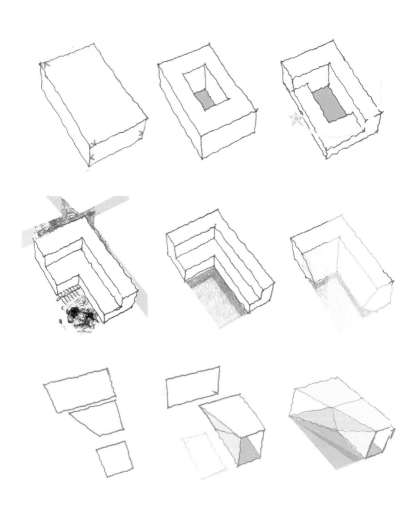

Apartment block massing
and facetation studies

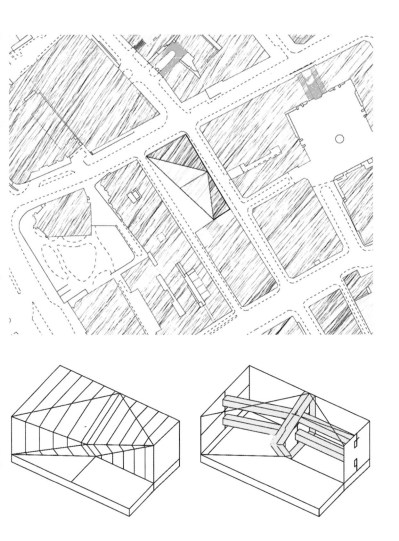

Top: Site plan

Bottom: Axonometric drawings of unit
subdivision and circulation system

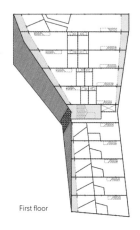

First floor

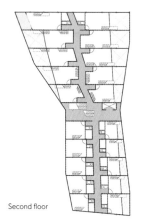

Second floor

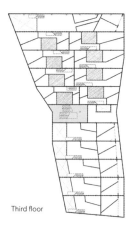

Third floor

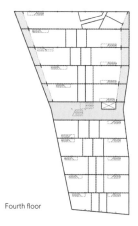

Fourth floor

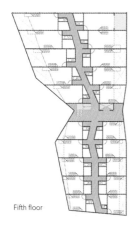

Fifth floor

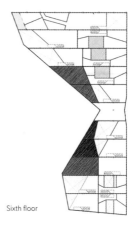

Sixth floor

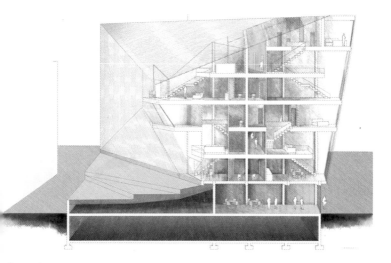

Cross section

Cladding detail:
perforated shading
using aluminium
skin panels

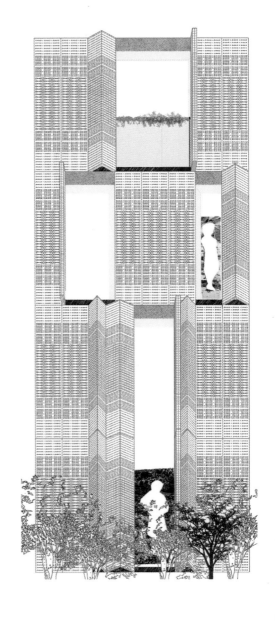

Floor plans,
apartment units

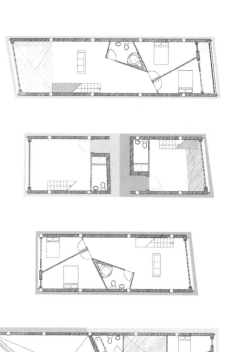

# CONCLUSION: THE DIGITAL VS PHYSICAL DEBATE

By reviewing the design studies presented here, a set of conclusions and discussion points arises. Many architects and architectural educators are very sceptical about such unconventional design methods, fearing the loss of design control, materiality, craftsmanship, functionality and relationship to context. They tend to blame generative-based design for all the negative aspects of contemporary architecture. However, the design method applied here proves them wrong. It manages to support a high degree of differentiation between the schemes, despite the fact that many of the projects were developed using the same techniques (e.g., triangulation). It also inevitably supports creativity and innovation, which is why so many of the projects managed to move beyond standard building typologies and layouts (e.g., the Porous Space project, page 80). Innovation emerged not only in formal design aspects, but also in terms of building programme and spatial solutions, offering new building-type hybridizations, such as the ferry terminal proposal on pages 108–15. The mix of different design tools and techniques, switching from traditional physical modelling, such as plaster casting, to advanced 3D printing and CNC fabrication, proved to be of great educational value (see pages 82–85). It offered students the opportunity to test materials with their hands, and to experience the advantages, difficulties and opportunities advanced technology has to offer – a design path that is often excluded, due to dogmatism or ignorance of (or lack of respect for) either handcrafting or computerized techniques. Neither banning computers nor abandoning traditional craftsmanship offers a solution for the future of architectural education.

Digital tools can often be seductive for designers. However, while speeding up the design process,

Generative
model iterations,
LSA final reviews

designing with digital tools makes gravity and materiality
disappear. Physical modelling helps designers and
students to reconnect with these two key elements,
which are so important for architectural production.
In addition, the switch between analogue and digital
tools allows students to filter out excess complexity
within a digitalized design process. By testing digital
findings with physical prototypes, they can begin
to assess whether a complex solution is really offering
spatial, aesthetic or programmatic qualities to a
project. The issue is not so much whether CAD and
3D modelling software should be banned or embraced
in undergraduate architectural education, but rather
to what extend they should be applied, in which
educational year and for what purpose. The same
principle applies for the use of digital fabrication.

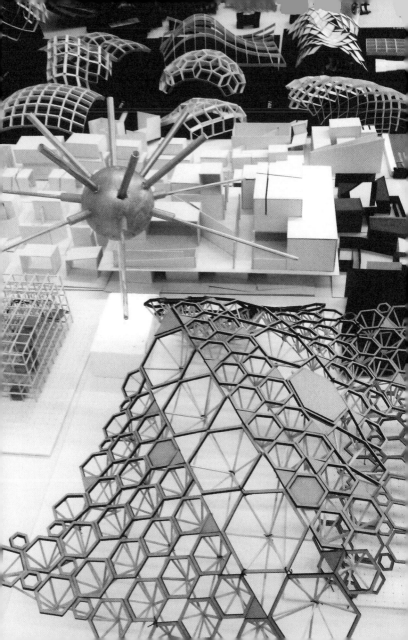

It is indeed irrational to apply such techniques to cutting out rectangular panels, but they are more than appropriate for mastering fabrication of complex geometries.

Alongside the loss of materiality and craftsmanship, many critics of generative design methods argue that the resulting architectural proposals are totally detached from their context. This is a criticism often applied to modern architecture as well. During our programme, the degree of integration or non-integration within a context was up to the designer. Building up a relationship between a building and its context can be achieved in many different ways. It can rely on form, materiality or programme, or all of the above. One can choose to harmonize, ignore or break with a building's context, a decision that does not depend on the design approach but on the designer's attitude towards the site. Nevertheless, external examiners overviewing the projects expressed surprise at the high degree of site-specific proposals, despite the unconventional design approach.

All of the finalized projects managed to comply with standards and requirements defined by the accreditation body (RIBA) and the module descriptors, as evident in the drawing and modelling outputs. In that sense, the generative design method applied proved highly appropriate for design education, helping students to develop their skills and self-confidence, and enhancing their future employability.

Looking at the difficulties accompanying such an approach, findings varied. Scepticism from other colleagues and fellow educators was definitely among them. This included guidance from tutors involved in the process as well as criticism from others observing the approach. From a student's point of view, the shift away from conventional design methods certainly appeared to be demanding. That became particularly evident after the completion of the form-finding phase; it was the Metamorphosis that presented the biggest challenges. As liberating and exciting as Morphogenesis might have been for some, abandoning the abstraction of the prototype and transforming it into a building proposal, overcoming obstacles of structure, urban context, planning and materiality seemed to be difficult. Many tended to start from scratch, leaving everything behind and following the conventional approach they were most familiar with. Some chose a brutal landing of their prototype into the site, without developing an attitude towards the context, while others failed to use their prototype for something more than simply trendy decoration.

Another issue that arose using this approach was having to manage the geometrical complexity that occurred. This was often a problem of representation. Complex geometries are easily produced in a digital environment, but controlling and representing their outputs often requires non-standardized methods as well. This can be a consequence of using software incorrectly, or of using inappropriate software for the task required. How can complex geometries be represented in floor plan, section and elevation? How can such geometries be built in a physical model?

This is when guidance is needed. Tutors play a critical role here. Educators need to guide students and enrich academic curricula with new design methods and tutored skills. But it is the student culture that plays an even more important role: the intercourse that occurs between students, either through daily procedures and presentations or through social media, websites and online forums. Today's young designers belong to a generation that has grown up with smartphones and computer tablets instead of crayons and paper, granting them familiarity with digital technologies from an early age. These are designers, therefore, who are more than able to deal with unconventional design methods, and who will hopefully revolutionize architectural production in the future.

Generative
model iterations,
LSA final reviews

# BIBLIOGRAPHY

Cappellato, G. *Mario Botta, Light and Gravity: Architecture 1993–2003*. Munich: Prestel, 2004.

Chilton, J. *Heinz Isler (Engineer's Contribution to Architecture)*. London: Thomas Telford, 2000.

Eisenman, P. *Eisenman Inside Out: Selected Writings 1963–1988 (Theoretical Perspectives in Architectural History & Criticism)*. New Haven: Yale University Press, 2004.

Frampton, K. *Studies in Tectonic Culture: The Poetics of Construction in Nineteenth and Twentieth Century Architecture*. Boston: MIT Press, 2001.

Haeckel, E. *Kunstformen der Natur*. 1904. Reprint, Wiesbaden: Marix Verlag, 2004.

Hensel, M., A. Menges and M. Weinstock. *Techniques and Technologies in Morphogenetic Design*. London: Wiley & Sons, 2006.

Jormakka, K. *Basics: Methoden der Formfindung*. Basel: Birkhäuser, 2007.

Khan-Magomedov, S. O. *Pioneers of Soviet Architecture: The Search for New Solutions in the 1920s and 1930s*. New York: Rizzoli, 1987.

Kolarevic, B. 'Digital Production.' In *Architecture in the Digital Age: Design and Manufacturing*, 46–48. London: Taylor & Francis, 2003.

Lazzeroni, C. (ed.), H. Bohnacker, B. Groß and J. Laub. *Generative Gestaltung: Entwerfen. Programmieren. Visualisieren. Mit internationalen Best-Practise-Beispielen, Grundlagen, Programmcodes und Ergebnissen*. Mainz: Schmidt Hermann, 2009.

Le Corbusier. *The Modulor*. 1948. Reprint, Basel: Birkhäuser, 2000.

Lynn, G. *Animate Form*. Princeton: Princeton Architectural Press, 1999.

Menocal, N. G., and R. Twombly. *Louis Sullivan: The Poetry of Architecture*. New York: W. W. Norton & Company, 2000.

Otto, F., and B. Rasch. *Finding Form: Towards an Architecture of the Minimal*. Stuttgart: Axel Menges, 1996.

Oxman, Rivka, and Richard Oxman. *Theories of the Digital in Architecture*. London: Routledge, 2013.

Soddu, C. 'The Design of Morphogenesis. An experimental research about the logical procedures in design processes.' *Demetra Magazine*, vol. 1, 1994.

Turnbull, J. *Toyo Ito: Generative Order (Kassler Lecturers)*. Princeton: Princeton Architectural Press, 2012.

Ungers, O. M. *O. M. Ungers: Morphologie/City Metaphors*. Manchester: Cornerhouse, 2011.

Van Berkel, B., and C. Bos (UNStudio). *Move: Imagination/Techniques/Effects*. 3-volume set. Amsterdam: Groose Press, 1999.

# INDEX

# INDEX

# PICTURE CREDITS

| | |
|---|---|
| Cover | Yiwei Gao, Man Jia, Xiao Lu, Yihan Zhang |
| 6–7 | Haoming Wang, Jingya Wu, Pengcheng Yao, Jiaxin Zhao |
| 11 | (Left) © Paul M.R. Maeyaert |
| | (Right) Asterios Agkathidis; © FLC / ADAGP, Paris and DACS, London 2015 |
| 13 | (Left) © Heritage Image Partnership Ltd / Alamy |
| | (Right) Asterios Agkathidis |
| 15 | © Vito Arcomano / Alamy |
| 18 | © VIEW Pictures Ltd / Alamy |
| 22–23 | Asterios Agkathidis |
| 24, 26–29 | Jianxuan Chen |
| 31 | Yuan Zhai |
| 32–33 | Xu Chen, Yuhui Qi, Peiyu Yang, Ruinan Zhang |
| 34–37 | Yuan Zhai |
| 39–41 | Jinglei Fu, Xiao Qi |
| 42–43 | Aqsa Imtiaz, Nadezda Kazakova, Xuerui Lu, Amy Whitmore |
| 44–45 | Nadezda Kazakova |
| 46–47 | Shimou Chen, Minhui Huang, Longfei Wang, Nan Yang, Yuan Zhai |
| 48, 50–53 | Xiao Gu, Yuedi Liu, Yangting Yang, Jinglei Fu, Wenxuan Zhang |
| 54–57 | Yuedi Liu |
| 59–61 | Shimou Chen, Longfei Wang, Nan Yang, Yuan Zhai |
| 62–63 | Charlotte Brookshouse, James Crookston, Minhui Huang, Lazaros Kyratsous |
| 64–69 | Yuan Zhai |
| 70–71 | Asterios Agkathidis |
| 73 | Sean Bailey |
| 74 | Asterios Agkathidis |
| 75 | David Barker, Sean Bailey |
| 76–79 | Sean Bailey |
| 81 | Yiqiang Zhao |
| 82–85 | Asterios Agkathidis |
| 86–89 | Yiqiang Zhao |
| 90–91 | Andrew Kent, Jiawei Liu, Boya Zhang |
| 92, 94–99 | Nojan Adami |
| 101 | Yiwei Gao, Man Jia, Xiao Lu, Yihan Zhang |
| 102–3 | Liang Gao, Jingchang Li |
| 104–7 | Yiwei Gao, Man Jia, Xiao Lu, Yihan Zhang |
| 108–15 | Man Jia |
| 116–17 | Haoming Wang, Jingya Wu, Pengcheng Yao, Jiaxin Zhao |
| 119–21 | Yuedi Liu, Yaoting Yang |
| 122–27 | Yuedi Liu |
| 128 | Emily Gayer, Tobi Griffiths, Michael Hill |
| 130–33 | Emily Gayer, Tobi Griffiths, Michael Hill |
| 134–39 | Yunxia Dai, Haochen Jia, Sen Lin, Jinhui Zhu |
| 140–45 | Emily Gayer |
| 146–47 | Asterios Agkathidis |
| 149–50 | Asterios Agkathidis |
| 153, 160 | Asterios Agkathidis |

# ACKNOWLEDGEMENTS

My grateful acknowledgements go to the Studio 04 tutors Richard Dod, Joanne Hudson, Mathew Wells, Howard Miller and Jane Moscardini for their enthusiasm and hard work, as well as the workshop team of Stuart Carroll, Michael Baldwin, Stephen Bretland and Aleksandar Kokai at the Liverpool School of Architecture.

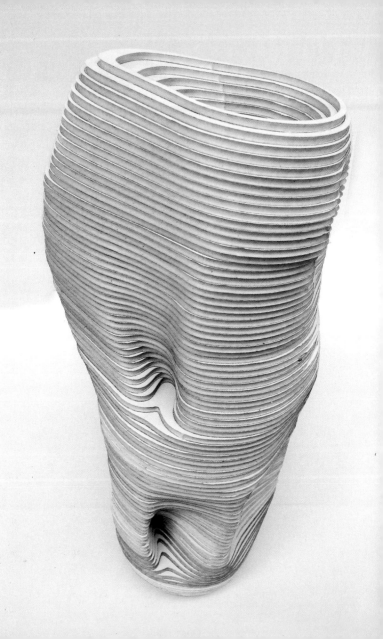